Healthy
Followers

SpiritBuilt Leadership 11

Malcolm Webber

Published by:

Strategic Press
www.StrategicPress.org

Strategic Press is a division of Strategic Global Assistance, Inc.
www.sgai.org

2601 Benham Avenue
Elkhart, IN 46517
U.S.A.

+1-574-295-4357
Toll-free: 888-258-7447

ISBN 978-1-888810-50-9

All Scripture references are from the New International Version of the Bible, unless otherwise noted.

Printed in the United States of America

Table of Contents

Introduction

This is a book about followers[1] – healthy ones. Healthy followers think and act.

Followers are often ignored when organizational successes or failures are explained. This is because:

1. Leaders are more visible than followers.

2. Considerably more study has been done on leadership than on "followership."

3. We suffer from significant misconceptions about the power of followers. Too often we look upon followers as fairly benign participants in the organization who remain passive until they receive instructions from their leader and then proceed, dutifully and unquestioningly, to follow those instructions.

As a result we do not sufficiently appreciate the contribution that effective followers actually do make to organizational success. To be effective themselves, leaders must have effective followers!

In this book we will study the often-neglected subject of healthy followers.

Malcolm Webber, Ph.D.
Elkhart Indiana

---

[1] In this book we have chosen to use the term "follower" simply because it is the one most commonly used by writers on this subject. We could just have easily have chosen terms like "constituent," "team member," "associate," "colleague," or "coworker." Certainly, we are equal coworkers, all followers of the one true Leader. We hope our choice of terms will not be offensive to anyone.

chapter 1

Healthy Followers

An understanding of followership is necessary in the discussion of leadership for several reasons:

1. Everyone – including leaders – is a follower at one time or another in their lives. Most individuals, even those in positions of high authority, have a supervisor of some kind. In fact, for many people it is not uncommon to switch between being a leader and being a follower several times during the course of a single day. For example, in an organization, middle managers answer to vice presidents, who answer to CEOs, who answer to boards of directors. Moreover, research on high-performance teams has demonstrated that the most successful teams are those that have a great deal of role switching among team members concerning who is serving in a leadership role at any given time.

2. The relationship of influence between leader and follower is not a one-way street. Leaders influence their followers, but they themselves are also influenced by those followers. Or, at least they should be. Unilateral, "one-way" leadership is usually abusive leadership, not healthy leadership. A healthy relationship between leader and follower involves a mutual exchange of influence. Effective followers enhance their leaders; unhealthy followers can undermine otherwise good leadership. Thus, we usually find the best leaders in the company of the most effective followers.

3. Few leaders can be effective without first having learned to be good followers. Many of the qualities that are desirable in a leader are also possessed by an effective follower. For example, most leaders would want their constituents to take

initiative, be capable of independent thought, be committed to a shared vision and common goals, and demonstrate self-giving courage. Furthermore, an effective follower will not only enthusiastically support and encourage his leader, but he will also be capable of respectfully challenging the leader if his actions threaten the vision or values of the organization. All these are leadership characteristics. Thus, a healthy leader with healthy followers will achieve their shared vision together.

4. To be both a good leader and a good follower is not easy. There is a great potential for role conflicts and ambiguities. Leaders are held responsible for everything that happens under their charge, but are also required to delegate much responsibility and authority to their constituents to empower them to act on their own. Leaders are also expected to teach and develop their followers which may involve building someone who will eventually take over part or all of the leader's own position, whether or not the leader is ready for that to happen. It is difficult to balance these competing and often conflicting demands and carry out the dual roles of leader and follower effectively.

Consequently, leaders need to understand effective followership so that they can be better followers and leaders themselves, and so they can help their constituents be better followers and leaders.

The popular conception that "everything depends on leadership" is not entirely correct. Without willing and effective followers, the greatest of leaders will fail.

> *The eye cannot say to the hand, "I don't need you!" And the head cannot say to the feet, "I don't need you!" On the contrary, those parts of the body that seem to be weaker are indispensable, (1 Cor. 12:21-22)*

chapter 2

Kinds of Followers

The definition of a healthy human body is one in which all the parts function properly. If one part of the body does not function properly we consider the body to be sick or disabled. It is the same in the Body of Christ. For the church – or any Christian ministry or organization – to grow to maturity and to fulfill her purpose in God, every member must function properly.

> *Instead, speaking the truth in love, we will in all things grow up into him who is the Head, that is, Christ. From him the whole body, joined and held together by every supporting ligament, grows and builds itself up in love, as each part does its work. (Eph. 4:15-16)*

For the vision of verse 15 to be fulfilled ("grow up into Him") the condition of verse 16 must be met ("each part does its work"). Thus, it is not sufficient for the church to have healthy leaders; we must also have healthy followers – those who take responsibility to function. A healthy follower takes two kinds of responsibilities: to think and to act.

In *The Power of Followership*, Robert Kelley describes five kinds of followers, categorized according to these two dimensions – thinking and acting.

Do You Think?

This first dimension is the quality of independent, critical thinking versus dependent, uncritical thinking:

- Independent, **critical thinkers** go beyond manuals and procedures. They consider the impact of their own actions and the actions of others, and they are willing to be creative and innovative and to offer constructive criticism when it is appropriate.

- Dependent, **uncritical thinkers** do not consider possibilities beyond what they are told, and do not contribute to the creative nurturing of the organization. They accept the leader's ideas without thinking, and they stick to the procedures or instructions – even when circumstances demand responsible deviation.

Do You Act?

The second dimension of follower style is active versus passive behavior:

- An **active** person demonstrates a sense of ownership. He participates fully in the organization, takes initiative in problem solving and decision making, interacts with coworkers at various levels, and goes beyond the bare necessities required by the job.

  > Go to the ant, you sluggard; consider its ways and be wise! It has no commander, no overseer or ruler, yet it stores its provisions in summer and gathers its food at harvest. (Prov. 6:6-8)

  > Like the coolness of snow at harvest time is a trustworthy messenger to those who send him; he refreshes the spirit of his masters. (Prov. 25:13)

- The **passive** individual needs constant supervision and encouragement by his supervisors. His level of involvement or interaction is limited to doing only what he is told to do. He avoids responsibilities beyond what the job specifically requires.

As vinegar to the teeth and smoke to the eyes, so is a sluggard to those who send him. (Prov. 10:26)

Like a bad tooth or a lame foot is reliance on the unfaithful in times of trouble. (Prov. 25:19; see also 26:10)

Do not be like the horse or the mule, which have no understanding but must be controlled by bit and bridle or they will not come to you. (Ps. 32:9)

The interaction of these two dimensions is shown in the following graphic, and determines whether the person is an alienated follower, a conformist, a passive follower, an effective follower, or a pragmatic survivor.

Kinds of Followers

Independent, critical thinking

Alienated	Effective

Passive   Pragmatic Survivor   Active

Passive	Conformist

Dependent, uncritical thinking

Source: Adapted from *The Power of Followership* by Robert E. Kelly

1. The **alienated follower** is a passive yet independent, critical thinker. He thinks but does not act. He is a "cynic." He may feel cheated or unappreciated by his organization. In the past he may have experienced setbacks or obstacles, perhaps promises broken by others. Often cynical in his attitude, the alienated follower is capable but unwilling to participate in nurturing the life of the organizational community. Usually he will dwell on the negatives and overlook the positives. Sadly, the alienated follower will often criticize the leader to others, without taking his complaints directly to the leader himself in a constructive, positive way.

2. The **conformist** participates actively in organizational life, but he is a dependent, uncritical thinker. He acts with little thought. The conformist is a "yes man," carrying out all orders without considering their consequences. In addition, he will frequently hide his weaknesses and cover his mistakes. His only concern is to avoid conflict. Authoritarian and abusive leaders prefer such followers. In addition, an organizational environment that is characterized by rigid rules that prohibit individual expression will suppress effective followership and lead to uncritical conformity.

3. The **passive follower** is a "sheep." He neither acts nor thinks. He is unenthusiastic and displays neither initiative nor a sense of responsibility. His activity is limited to what he is specifically told to do, and he accomplishes things only with a great deal of supervision. He leaves all the thinking to his leaders. Leaders who dominate and control their people and who punish mistakes often create such followers who are afraid to think or to take responsible action.

4. The **effective follower** is both a critical, independent thinker and active in the organization. Thinking and acting, he is a true "coworker." Fundamentally committed to a purpose outside himself, he works creatively and enthusiastically

14

toward achieving the organizational community's goals. He is not afraid of taking intelligent risks; neither does he shy away from necessary conflicts. He has the courage to initiate change in the best interests of all.

Such followers are essential for the organization to be effective. They are capable of self-leadership, they discern strengths and weaknesses in themselves and others, they are committed to the shared vision, and they work toward its fulfillment with energy, innovation and responsibility that are contagious. With such constituents, the church or ministry will experience a healthy "fit" between the community vision and the individual visions.

An unhealthy community:
strong individual purposes without any overarching, unifying corporate purpose

An unhealthy community:
strong corporate purpose without contributing individual purposes

An unhealthy community:
individual purposes are not aligned with the corporate purpose

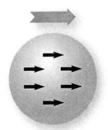

A healthy community:
strong individual purposes are aligned with overarching, unifying corporate purpose

5. The **pragmatic survivor** has qualities of all four extremes, depending on which style aligns best with the prevailing situation. He is somewhat of a "politician." Perpetually testing the wind, he will use whatever style benefits his own agenda and minimizes risk. Within any given organization, 25 to 35 percent of the people tend to be pragmatic survivors. On the positive side, when the organization is going through difficult times such a follower may make a positive contribution since he knows "how to work the system to get things done." Negatively, this same behavior can be interpreted – often correctly – as "playing political games," or adjusting to maximize his own self-interest.

Self-Evaluation Exercise:

For each question,[2] please use the five-point scale to indicate the extent to which the statements describe you. Think of a specific but typical followership situation and how you acted.

1	2	3	4	5
Rarely		Occasionally		Almost Always

_____ 1. Does your role in the organization help you fulfill your own personal vision or dream that is important to you?

_____ 2. Are your personal work goals aligned with the organization's specific goals?

_____ 3. Are you highly committed to the organization? Are you energized by your work? Do you labor with passion and give your very best ideas and performance?

_____ 4. Are you so enthusiastic that your energy and zeal spread to your coworkers?

_____ 5. Instead of passively waiting for or merely accepting what the leader tells you, do you personally identify which activities are the most critical for achieving the organization's goals?

_____ 6. Do you actively develop your own competencies in those critical activities so that you become more valuable to the leader and to the organization?

_____ 7. When starting a new job or assignment, do you immediately begin to build a record of successes in tasks that are important to the leader?

---

[2] These questions are adapted from *The Power of Followership* by Robert Kelley. For an online version, please go to: www.leadersource.org/ /resources/ instruments/

_____ 8. Can your leader give you a difficult assignment without the benefit of much supervision, confident that you will accomplish it with timely and high quality work and that you will "figure it out" as necessary?

_____ 9. Do you take the initiative to seek out and accomplish assignments that are beyond your normal job responsibilities?

_____ 10. When you are not the formal leader of a particular group project, do you still contribute at a high level, often doing more than your share?

_____ 11. Do you independently think up and promote creative new ideas that will contribute significantly to the leader's or organization's goals?

_____ 12. Do you give your very best effort to solve the tough problems with God's help, rather than look to the leader to do it for you?

_____ 13. Do you look for opportunities to help your coworkers, making them succeed, even when you will not get any credit?

_____ 14. Do you try to help the leader or group see both the potential benefits and risks of ideas or plans, constructively playing the "devil's advocate" as necessary?

_____ 15. Do you consciously try to understand the leader's needs, goals and limitations, and work hard to meet them?

_____ 16. Do you try to anticipate upcoming problems to solve them in advance, rather than waiting for the leader to tell you what to prepare for?

_____ 17. Do you actively, openly and honestly acknowledge your own strengths and weaknesses rather than avoid evaluation and accountability?

_____ 18. Do you internally question the leader's decisions when necessary, rather than just doing what you are told?

_____ 19. Do you act on your conscience according to biblical standards, rather than the leader's or group's standards?

_____ 20. Do you humbly and kindly assert your views on important issues, even though they might not be received by the leader or the group?

SCORING:

Questions 1, 5, 11, 12, 14, 16, 17, 18, 19, and 20 measure independent, critical thinking. Total your answers and write your score below:

Independent Critical Thinking Total Score = _____

Questions 2, 3, 4, 6, 7, 8, 9, 10, 13, and 15 measure active engagement. Total your answers and write your score below:

Active Engagement Total Score = _____

EVALUATION:

The two scores indicate what kind of follower you are, according to each dimension:

- 20 or below is low.
- Between 20 and 40 is in the middle.
- 40 or above is high.

Based on whether your scores are low, middle or high in each of these areas, please assess your follower style:

Kind of Follower	Independent, Critical Thinking Score	Active Engagement Score
Effective	High	High
Alienated	High	Low
Conformist	Low	High
Pragmatic Survivor	Middle	Middle
Passive	Low	Low

PLEASE ANSWER THE FOLLOWING QUESTIONS:

1. What kind of follower are you?
2. Why are you this way?
3. What can you do to be a more effective follower?

chapter 3

Characteristics of Healthy Followers

Our goal is healthy churches and Christian ministries. This means every member must take responsibility for the whole; every member must function actively and thoughtfully:

> *From him the whole body, joined and held together by every supporting ligament, grows and builds itself up in love, as each part does its work. (Eph. 4:16)*

The following are eleven characteristics of active, thoughtful followers[3]:

1. **Obey.** God has established our leaders in their roles so that we can follow them.

    > *Obey your leaders and submit to their authority. They keep watch over you as men who must give an account. Obey them so that their work will be a joy, not a burden, for that would be of no advantage to you. (Heb. 13:17)*

    This should not be:

    - the grudging, sometimes subversive, obedience of the alienated follower,
    - the mindless obedience of the conformist,
    - the bare-minimum, unenthusiastic obedience of the passive sheep, or

---

[3] Of course, these are also characteristics of healthy leaders in their relationships with other leaders.

- the manipulative, self-serving obedience of the pragmatic survivor.

It should be an obedience that is both thoughtful and active.

> ...obey your earthly masters in everything; and do it, not only when their eye is on you and to win their favor, but with sincerity of heart and reverence for the Lord. Whatever you do, work at it with all your heart, as working for the Lord, not for men, since you know that you will receive an inheritance from the Lord as a reward. It is the Lord Christ you are serving. (Col. 3:22-24)

> ...obey your earthly masters with respect and fear, and with sincerity of heart, just as you would obey Christ. Obey them not only to win their favor when their eye is on you, but like slaves of Christ, doing the will of God from your heart. Serve wholeheartedly, as if you were serving the Lord, not men, because you know that the Lord will reward everyone for whatever good he does, whether he is slave or free. (Eph. 6:5-8)

2. **Encourage.** During normal times, the leader carries the burden of responsibility for the entire organization

> Besides everything else, I face daily the pressure of my concern for all the churches. Who is weak, and I do not feel weak? Who is led into sin, and I do not inwardly burn? (2 Cor. 11:28-29)

In addition, all leaders go through difficult times. Perhaps the leader is trying to bring needed change to the organization and is encountering resistance. During such times, a healthy follower will actively look for ways to express support and encouragement to his leader.

I was glad when Stephanas, Fortunatus and Achaicus arrived, because they have supplied what was lacking from you. For they refreshed my spirit and yours also. Such men deserve recognition. (1 Cor. 16:17-18)

May the Lord show mercy to the household of Onesiphorus, because he often refreshed me and was not ashamed of my chains. (2 Tim. 1:16)

Your love has given me great joy and encouragement, because you, brother, have refreshed the hearts of the saints. (Philem. 7)

He who tends a fig tree will eat its fruit, and he who looks after his master will be honored. (Prov. 27:18)

There are many ways such encouragement can be given: through notes, cards, children's pictures, food, gifts, personal visits. Just a word spoken at the right time can be of great encouragement to a leader:

...how good is a timely word! (Prov. 15:23)

A word aptly spoken is like apples of gold in settings of silver. (Prov. 25:11)

3. **Take responsibility.** Effective followers take responsibility for the success of the whole organization, not just their own areas. Consequently, they will take the initiative to do what is necessary without being told. In addition, they will go beyond their normal duties when appropriate. They actively look for ways to make a positive impact. When serious problems arise, they will point out the problems to the leader and suggest solutions. Healthy followers will see themselves as participants and not mere spectators in the processes of organizational health and growth. Thus, paradoxically, the key to being an

effective follower is the ability to think for oneself – to exercise control and independence and to work without close supervision.

> *Go to the ant, you sluggard; consider its ways and be wise! It has no commander, no overseer or ruler, yet it stores its provisions in summer and gathers its food at harvest. (Prov. 6:6-8)*

> *locusts have no king, yet they advance together in ranks; (Prov. 30:27)*

Ineffective followers, on the other hand, allow themselves to be dominated by the hierarchy and, seeing themselves as subservient, vacillate between despair over their seeming powerlessness and attempts to manipulate leaders for their own purposes. Either their fear of powerlessness becomes a self-fulfilling prophecy or their resentment leads them to undermine the organization's effectiveness.

4. **Give advice and counsel.** The leader does not have all the answers, especially when he is new or inexperienced. Secure leaders build mutually trusting relationships with capable followers who look for opportunities to provide helpful advice, ask questions, or simply to be good listeners when the situation demands it. Sometimes leaders will be hesitant about asking for such input; it becomes the follower's responsibility to take the initiative to offer his help. In addition, the healthy follower will maintain this relationship with absolute confidentiality and refuse to boast to others about his special relationship with his leader or the "inside knowledge" he is sometimes privy to. Furthermore, he will not nag his leader even when he is certain he knows better.

> *Instruct a wise man and he will be wiser still; teach a righteous man and he will add to his learning. (Prov. 9:9)*

Plans fail for lack of counsel, but with many advisers they succeed. (Prov. 15:22; see also 24:6)

5. **Challenge when necessary.** When there are potential drawbacks or problems with a leader's plans or ideas, a healthy follower will bring these issues to light.

Such challenges can be negative ("you're wrong…") or positive ("you're right but we can do this even better…").

> *…rebuke a wise man and he will love you. Instruct a wise man and he will be wiser still; teach a righteous man and he will add to his learning. (Prov. 9:8-9; see also 17:10; 19:25; 27:5-6)*

In Exodus 18, Jethro challenged Moses' leadership practice and the resulting structural change was good for everyone.

> *"If you do this and God so commands, you will be able to stand the strain, and all these people will go home satisfied." Moses listened to his father-in-law and did everything he said. (Ex. 18:23-24)*

Ruth made a passionate appeal to Naomi that won her heart and eventually a spouse.

> *"Look," said Naomi, "your sister-in-law is going back to her people and her gods. Go back with her." But Ruth replied, "Don't urge me to leave you or to turn back from you. Where you go I will go, and where you stay I will stay. Your people will be my people and your God my God. Where you die I will die, and there I will be buried. May the LORD deal with me, be it ever so severely, if anything but death separates you and me." When Naomi realized that Ruth was determined to go with her, she stopped urging her. (Ruth 1:15-18)*

In Galatians 2, Paul challenged certain leaders' treatment of the Gentile believers and the result was the preservation of truth in the church.

> *We did not give in to them for a moment, so that the truth of the gospel might remain with you. (Gal. 2:5)*

Naturally, one must challenge a leader in the right way; leaders often get defensive in response to negative feedback. An appropriate manner for raising concerns includes:

- Being sure it really matters. Don't challenge a leader over every little thing!
- Having a history of submission and cooperation.
- Praying first for grace, wisdom and favor.
- Acknowledging the leader's position and right to make the final decision.
- Communicating a sincere desire to help the leader fulfill the organization's purpose. If the leader senses that the follower has a personal agenda, he will be unlikely to listen (Prov. 28:25a).
- Pointing out specifics rather than vague generalities.
- Refraining from personalizing the critique.
- Avoiding threats of non-compliance if the leader does not take heed.[4]

The leader must never forget that the follower's loyalty is not to him but to the Lord Jesus and to the purposes of God for the organization. Frequently, leaders misinterpret their followers' commitment. Seeing their own authority acknowledged, they mistake loyalty to God and His will for loyalty to themselves. The reality is that we are all coworkers in the purposes of God;

---

[4] Certainly, there may be times when the follower absolutely could not follow a particular path; for example, when clear ethical or legal issues are involved (see point 11). Most of the time, however, threats of non-compliance are inappropriate and counter-productive.

thus, no one of us is above challenge and accountability.

6. **Seek honest feedback.** It can be difficult for a leader to express negative concerns about a follower's weaknesses. It is much easier to focus only on his strengths. To build mutual trust and openness, a healthy follower will encourage the leader to be candid and direct. He will ask the leader for input on how his performance can be more effective, and he will not withdraw and sulk when the leader shares corrections or concerns.

> *He who heeds discipline shows the way to life, but whoever ignores correction leads others astray. (Prov. 10:17)*

> *Whoever loves discipline loves knowledge, but he who hates correction is stupid. (Prov. 12:1)*

> *The way of a fool seems right to him, but a wise man listens to advice. (Prov. 12:15; see also 4:1; 5:11-14; 13:1, 10, 13, 18; 15:5, 10, 12, 31-32; 16:20; 17:10)*

In this way, the healthy follower chooses accountability regarding his own life, the details of his own ministry and how his ministry fits with the whole community.

7. **Clarify roles and expectations.** It is the leader's responsibility to make known to his followers what their exact roles and responsibilities are. Nevertheless, many leaders fail to communicate these things:

- Clear job expectations.
- Scope of authority and responsibility.
- Specific goals that must be attained.
- Deadlines.

Followers must pursue clarification in these areas. Sometimes the issue is role conflict: the leader directs a follower to perform mutually exclusive tasks and expects results from all of them at the same time. Healthy followers will diplomatically but firmly resolve role ambiguity and conflict.

8. **Show appreciation.** Healthy leaders affirm their followers, and healthy followers affirm their leaders. When such affirmation is sincere and not manipulative, it will strengthen the leader-follower relationship as well as encourage the leader to push ahead toward the fulfillment of the vision.

> *He threw himself at Jesus' feet and thanked him – and he was a Samaritan. Jesus asked, "Were not all ten cleansed? Where are the other nine? Was no one found to return and give praise to God except this foreigner?" (Luke 17:16-18)*

> *We have spoken freely to you, Corinthians, and opened wide our hearts to you. We are not withholding our affection from you, but you are withholding yours from us. As a fair exchange – I speak as to my children – open wide your hearts also. (2 Cor. 6:11-13)*

9. **Keep the leader informed.** Leaders rely on their followers to keep them informed about many aspects of the life and activity of the organization.

> *My brothers, some from Chloe's household have informed me that there are quarrels among you. (1 Cor. 1:11)*

> *It is actually reported that there is sexual immorality among you... (1 Cor. 5:1)*

> *You learned it from Epaphras, our dear fellow servant, who is a faithful minister of Christ on our behalf, and who also told us of your love in the Spirit. (Col. 1:7-8)*

But Timothy has just now come to us from you and has brought good news about your faith and love. He has told us that you always have pleasant memories of us and that you long to see us, just as we also long to see you. (1 Thess. 3:6)

Without accurate and timely information, a leader cannot make good decisions since he will lack a complete picture of what is happening. Leaders who appear not to know what is going on will feel and look incompetent; it is embarrassing for a leader to hear from others about events or changes taking place within his sphere of authority. Followers must share both positive and negative information with their leaders; those who "protect" the leader by withholding negative information sabotage the entire organization. Exactly how much and how often you should inform the leader about issues are complex matters. A leader cannot, and should not, be aware of all the details in an organization. Finding the right balance is much easier when there is a relationship of mutual trust and respect.

10. **Verify accuracy.** It is extremely important that the follower verify the accuracy of information he passes along to the leader. Rumors, complaints and reports of problems can have a disproportionate effect if the leader assumes incorrectly that the follower took the time to substantiate them.

    Kings take pleasure in honest lips; they value a man who speaks the truth. (Prov. 16:13)

    Moreover, the good follower will not pretend to know more than he really does when asked about a given situation, preferring instead to defer his answer until he has had a chance to find out.

    …What you have seen with your eyes do not bring hastily to court, for what will you do in the end if your neighbor puts you to shame? (Prov. 25:7-8)

Do you see a man who speaks in haste? There is more hope for a fool than for him. (Prov. 29:20; see also 10:18b; 12:17; 13:3; 14:5, 25; 15:7, 28)

11. **Resist inappropriate influence.** The healthy follower knows he is not required by God to comply with instructions to do what is abusive, illegal or unethical, or to believe what is theologically aberrant. He will not sacrifice the purpose of the organization or his own integrity just to maintain harmony and minimize conflict.

> *But Daniel resolved not to defile himself with the royal food and wine, and he asked the chief official for permission not to defile himself this way. (Dan. 1:8)*

> *Shadrach, Meshach and Abednego replied to the king, "O Nebuchadnezzar, we do not need to defend ourselves before you in this matter. If we are thrown into the blazing furnace, the God we serve is able to save us from it, and he will rescue us from your hand, O king. But even if he does not, we want you to know, O king, that we will not serve your gods or worship the image of gold you have set up." (Dan. 3:16-18)*

> *Then they called them in again and commanded them not to speak or teach at all in the name of Jesus. But Peter and John replied, "Judge for yourselves whether it is right in God's sight to obey you rather than God. For we cannot help speaking about what we have seen and heard." (Acts 4:18-20)*

> *Having brought the apostles, they made them appear before the Sanhedrin to be questioned by the high priest. "We gave you strict orders not to teach in this name," he said. "Yet you have filled Jerusalem with your teaching and are determined to make us guilty of this man's blood."*

Peter and the other apostles replied: "We must obey God rather than men!" (Acts 5:27-29)

When Peter came to Antioch, I opposed him to his face, because he was clearly in the wrong. (Gal. 2:11)

First, in a firm but tactful way, he should remind the leader of his own spiritual and ethical responsibilities, pointing out the negative consequences of the proposed course of action.[5]

Through patience a ruler can be persuaded, and a gentle tongue can break a bone. (Prov. 25:15)

Second, he should attempt to hold the leader accountable within the authority structure of the organization. If his attempts at bringing correction fail, he may need to leave the organization. At all times, he must retain the right spirit and not become personally hostile.

Self-Evaluation Exercise:

Think of a relationship in which you are or were a "follower." Please answer each question[6] about your own behavior using the scale of 1 to 5, where 1 means you do not do it, and 5 means you do it regularly.

Then, using the same scale, ask your *immediate* leader or overseer how he or she would assess your behavior. Be sure to give them genuine permission to be open and honest with you.

---

[5] For more on how to make an appeal to an authority figure please see chapter 16 of *The Christian Family* by Malcolm Webber.

[6] These questions are adapted from *Leadership: Theory, Application, Skill Development* by Lussier & Achua. For an online version, please go to: www.leadersource.org/ /resources/instruments/

Specific Behavior	Your Own Assessment of Yourself					Your Immediate Leader's Assessment of You				
1. From my heart, I willingly choose to obey my leader and to loyally follow his direction.	1 No	2	3	4	5 Yes	1 No	2	3	4	5 Yes
2. When things are not going well, I go out of my way to encourage and support my leader.	1 No	2	3	4	5 Yes	1 No	2	3	4	5 Yes
3. I look for ways in which I can take the initiative to do more than my normal job requires, and I do this without being asked.	1 No	2	3	4	5 Yes	1 No	2	3	4	5 Yes
4. I give my leader advice when it is appropriate; for example, if he is new and inexperienced or if he needs help in a difficult situation.	1 No	2	3	4	5 Yes	1 No	2	3	4	5 Yes
5. When my leader makes a poor decision, I share my concerns with him and try to help him improve the decision; I do not simply implement it.	1 No	2	3	4	5 Yes	1 No	2	3	4	5 Yes

Specific Behavior	Your Own Assessment of Yourself					Your Immediate Leader's Assessment of You				
6. I genuinely encourage my leader to give me candid feedback on how I'm doing, rather than avoiding it and becoming defensive when it is offered.	1 No	2	3	4	5 Yes	1 No	2	3	4	5 Yes
7. I actively try to understand my role in tasks by clarifying my leader's expectations of me and my performance standards.	1 No	2	3	4	5 Yes	1 No	2	3	4	5 Yes
8. I warmly show my appreciation to my leader; for example, by thanking him when he does something in my best interest.	1 No	2	3	4	5 Yes	1 No	2	3	4	5 Yes
9. I intentionally keep my leader informed, including about bad news. I do not wait for him to ask me about things.	1 No	2	3	4	5 Yes	1 No	2	3	4	5 Yes
10. I diligently verify the accuracy of the information I give my leader.	1 No	2	3	4	5 Yes	1 No	2	3	4	5 Yes

Specific Behavior	Your Own Assessment of Yourself					Your Immediate Leader's Assessment of You				
11. If my leader were to ask me to do something illegal or unethical, I would resist such an instruction in an appropriate manner.	1 No	2	3	4	5 Yes	1 No	2	3	4	5 Yes

Add the totals in each column.		

SCORING:

The higher your score, the more effective you are as a follower.

55: You're an awesome follower and a sheer joy to have on the team!

45-54: You're doing very well.

35-44: You're not doing too badly but you do need to improve in certain areas.

25-34: You've got some serious attitude adjustments to make.

15-24: It's a wonder your boss can put up with you!

PLEASE ANSWER THE FOLLOWING QUESTIONS:

1. Are you surprised by your own overall score?
2. Are you surprised by your leader's assessment of your behavior?
3. Does your own assessment differ significantly from your leader's assessment? If so, why?
4. Were you strong in some areas and weak in others? If so, which ones?

5. What are your specific plans for personal improvement as a follower?
6. Please ask your leader to tell you specific ways that you could improve. What are his or her suggestions?

chapter 4

How Followers Influence Their Organizations

Elsewhere we have defined "leadership power" as the leader's *capacity to influence others to move* from where they are now to somewhere else.[7]

Formally, leaders have more organizational power than do followers. Nevertheless, good followers do exercise considerable power to positively influence the direction and effectiveness of the organization.

All followers have two potential kinds of power: personal and position-based.

1. The follower possesses various **personal** sources of power:

    *   Specific *education, knowledge, skills* and *expertise.*
    *   *Energy* to learn, accept undesirable projects, and to take responsibility beyond the boundaries of his job description.
    *   *Relationships* by which he can persuade others (including leaders) to move in the right direction.

    All these can be valuable resources to the organization when used correctly.

2. Often the **position** of a follower in an organization can provide sources of power:

---

[7] Please see *Leadership: SpiritBuilt Leadership #1* by Malcolm Webber.

- His *responsibilities* may cause him to interact with many people.
- A *central location* provides influence because he is known to many and is directly involved in the work of many.
- A position that is central to the *flow of information* will be a very influential one.
- Through his *network of relationships* the follower has great opportunity to persuade others and to make significant contributions to the success of the organization.

Thus, there are many ways in which healthy followers can influence the direction and success of their organizations.

chapter 5

How Followers Influence Their Leaders

At some point, most followers complain about their leaders. Some of the most common complaints are:

- "My leader will not listen to me."
- "He will not encourage me."
- "He will not recognize my efforts."[8]

Apart from the Lord Jesus, no leader will ever be perfect. All leaders can, however, improve in their leadership. Followers can actually help their leaders improve by doing the following:

1. **Overcome the barrier.** Most relationships between leaders and followers are characterized by certain degrees of emotion and behavior based on authority and submission. A leader is an authority figures and may play a disproportionately large role in the mind of a follower. Followers may find themselves being overcritical of the leader, or rebellious, or passive. Some leader-follower relationships are similar to parent-child relationships, and people may find themselves engaging in old family patterns when relating to their leaders. Healthy followers will understand that we are all one in Christ:

   There is neither Jew nor Greek, slave nor free, male nor

---

[8] Len Schlesinger, "It Doesn't Take a Wizard to Build a Better Boss," *Fast Company,* June/July 1996, pp. 102-107.

female, for you are all one in Christ Jesus. (Gal. 3:28)

In Christ we are all equal; thus, followers are not inherently subordinate. With this perspective, we can all relate well to our leaders, while maintaining the appropriate respect.

2. **Be realistic.** The healthy follower has given up idealized images of his leader and knows that all leaders are fallible and make mistakes. This acceptance of the leader's humanity is the foundation of a healthy relationship. We must view our leaders as they really are; not as we think they should be or would like them to be.

> *What, after all, is Apollos? And what is Paul? Only servants, through whom you came to believe – as the Lord has assigned to each his task. (1 Cor. 3:5)*

In addition, good followers will present realistic images of themselves. They will not try to hide their weaknesses or cover their mistakes. Neither will they criticize their leaders to others; instead they will directly and constructively disagree with them.

3. **Strive to understand.** The healthy follower will go to lengths to understand his leader, asking such questions as:

- What is the leader trying to accomplish in the long-term?
- What are his short-term goals?
- What does the leader want me to accomplish – and how does that relate to question #1?
- Why is the leader in charge? Why did God choose this person for this position?
- Does my vision line up with the leader's vision?
- Do my goals advance the leader's vision – or conflict with it?

- What kinds of problems most worry the leader?
- What kinds of victories most please the leader?
- What past experiences has the leader been through that have made him the way he is now?
- What pressures and challenges does the leader face now?
- What strengths do I have that can complement the leader's weaknesses?

4. **Build a relationship.** Based upon trust and open, honest communication, healthy followers will build strong and genuine relationships with their leaders. This two-way relationship will be characterized more by mutual respect than by formal authority and hierarchy.

> *He who loves a pure heart and whose speech is gracious will have the king for his friend. (Prov. 22:11; see also Eccl. 4:9-12)*

Leaders need friends. Christian leaders never grow to the point where they no longer need vital relationships with others around them. Effective Christian leaders lead in a context of community – not as tough "ministry islands" off by themselves. In the body of Christ, no members are independent (1 Cor. 12).

Jesus had friends (Matt. 26:36-38); how much more do we need friends!

Paul, the great apostle, also had friends:

> *I was glad when Stephanas, Fortunatus and Achaicus arrived, because they have supplied what was lacking from you. For they refreshed my spirit and yours also. Such men deserve recognition. (1 Cor. 16:17-18)*

These men traveled a long distance to minister to Paul. Notably, Stephanas was Paul's own convert (v. 15)! However, he did not allow any distance to come between him and his dear friend Paul but took the initiative to seek him out in his time of need (cf. 2 Tim. 1:16-18).

A close reading of Romans 16:1-16 show the depth of friendship that Paul enjoyed with a number of saints. The passage mentions several of Paul's "beloved" friends and even a "spiritual mother" in verse 16!

Like Jesus and Paul, leaders need friends.

5. **Be a resource.** Effective followers align themselves with the purposes of the organization. They understand their potential impact on the organization's success or failure. They ask the leader about the vision and goals so they can help achieve them. They invite the leader to share about his experiences – both good and bad – in the organization's history. They openly discuss their own personal goals and resources that they can contribute to the organization. They are candid about their weaknesses and constraints. In these ways, followers become sources of strength for their leaders.

    Do you see a man skilled in his work? He will serve before kings; he will not serve before obscure men. (Prov. 22:29)

6. **Help the leader improve.** Followers can help their leaders become better leaders in a number of ways:

    - The follower who asks the leader for advice will help the leader to give it. If a leader senses that his input is well-regarded and desired, he will be more likely to give effective counsel rather than unsympathetic criticism.
    - The follower who tells the leader what he needs in order to succeed will help the leader know what to give him.

- The follower who compliments and thanks the leader for treating him well will reinforce such behavior.
- The follower who is honest when the leader is counter-productive will help him recognize the need for change.

If a ruler's anger rises against you, do not leave your post; calmness can lay great errors to rest. (Eccl. 10:4)

Conclusion

In these days, God is building new spiritual communities in churches and Christian organizations. The traditional formal barriers between leader ("clergy") and follower ("laity") are being broken down. Ministry teams are being formed based upon mutual respect and shared leadership. The people are being mobilized and empowered.

Nevertheless, we still have leaders – and we will always have them. This is the way God has made mankind. But our leaders are changing as our understanding of their role changes first.

For the church of Jesus Christ to accomplish His purposes these radical changes must continue. Our leaders must be honest and transparent – true servants of God and His people. The people must be passionate and whole-hearted in their ministries as we all work together to fulfill the shared vision of His glory.

Everything does not rise or fall merely on leadership; the whole body must function and it must function in a healthy manner.

From him the whole body, joined and held together by every supporting ligament, grows and builds itself up in love, as each part does its work. (Eph. 4:16)

Selected Bibliography

Chaleff, Ira. *The Courageous Follower: Standing Up to and for Our Leaders (2nd ed.).* San Francisco, CA: Berrett-Koehler Publishers. 2003.

Daft, Richard L. *Leadership: Theory and Practice.* Orlando, FL: The Dryden Press. 1999.

Kelley, Robert E. *The Power of Followership: How to Create Leaders People Want to Follow and Followers Who Lead Themselves.* New York: Doubleday/Currency. 1992.

Lussier, Robert & Christopher Achua. *Leadership: Theory, Application, Skill Development.* Cincinnati, OH: South-Western College Publishing. 2001.

Rosenbach, William E. & Robert L. Taylor (eds.). *Contemporary Issues in Leadership (4th ed.).* Boulder, CO: Westview Press. 1998.

Yukl, Gary. *Leadership in Organizations (4th ed.).* Upper Saddle River, NJ: Prentice Hall. 1998.

Books in the *SpiritBuilt Leadership* Series
by Malcolm Webber, Ph.D.

1. *Leadership.* Deals with the nature of leadership, servant leadership, and other basic leadership issues.

2. *Healthy Leaders.* Presents a simple but effective model of what constitutes a healthy Christian leader.

3. *Leading.* A study of the practices of exemplary leaders.

4. *Building Leaders.* Leaders build leaders! However, leader development is highly complex and very little understood. This book examines core principles of leader development.

5. *Leaders & Managers.* Deals with the distinctions between leaders and managers. Contains extensive worksheets.

6. *Abusive Leadership.* A must read for all Christian leaders. Reveals the true natures and sources of abusive leadership and servant leadership.

7. *Understanding Change.* Leading change is one of the most difficult leadership responsibilities. It is also one of the most important. This book is an excellent primer that will help you understand resistance to change, the change process and how to help people through change.

8. *Building Teams.* What teams are and how they best work.

9. *Understanding Organizations.* A primer on organizational structure.

10. *Women in Leadership.* A biblical study concerning this very controversial issue.

11. **Healthy Followers.** The popular conception that "everything depends on leaders" is not entirely correct. Without thoughtful and active followers, the greatest of leaders will fail. This book studies the characteristics of healthy followers and is also a great resource for team building.

12. **Listening.** Listening is one of the most important of all leadership skills. This book studies how we can be better listeners and better leaders.

13. **Transformational Thinking.** This book introduces a new model of transformational thinking – of loving God with our minds – that identifies the critical thinking capacities of a healthy Christian leader. In addition, practical ways of nurturing those thinking capacities are described.

Strategic Press
www.StrategicPress.org

Strategic Press is a division of Strategic Global Assistance, Inc.
www.sgai.org

2601 Benham Avenue
Elkhart, IN 46517
U.S.A.

+1-574-295-4357
Toll-free: 888-258-7447

LaVergne, TN USA
26 May 2010
184081LV00004B/2/P

9 781888 810509